Safety in Numbers

Safety in Numbers

The heavy business of Life Assurance made light, instructive and readable

Tessa Morrison

Illustrated by Arthur Robins

Hutchinson Benham, London

Life assurance is a complicate

It's all too easy to fill a book or
jargon and figures.

This book offers an alternativ

usiness.

t with diagrams, regulations,

approach.

This book was sponsored by the
Provident Mutual Life Assurance Association,
25-31 Moorgate, London EC2,
and conceived by PVA Advertising

Hutchinson Benham Ltd, 3 Fitzroy Square, London W1P 6JD

An imprint of the Hutchinson Group

London Melbourne Sydney Auckland Wellington Johannesburg and
agencies throughout the world

First published 1978

Photoset in Century Schoolbook by Owl Creative Services Ltd

Printed in Great Britain by The Anchor Press Ltd and bound by
Wm Brendon, both of Tiptree, Essex

ISBN 0 09 134181 7

Contents

Introduction: United we stand

Imagine a caveman wanted life assurance, what would he do?

He'd either give a cavewoman a wink and start a family, or else take refuge in the local tribe. Even the earliest *homo sapiens* soon realized that the best way to face life's dangers was together.

Mind you, a visiting life assurance salesman might have put a few ideas into his head:

These salesmen were very keen on the group idea, especially when it came to bison. 'Terrific combination of protection and investment elements here', they would say, as salesmen do. 'Beats fossils by a long chalk.'

The Bison Insurance Plan went something like this:

HUNTER WITH BISON...

...SHARES IT AROUND...

...SO THAT WHEN HE'S WITHOUT BISON...

... HE GETS HIS SHARE FROM SOMEONE ELSE.

It was simply a pooling of resources, very similar in fact to life assurance as we know it today. We of the Jet Age still club together like those of the Stone Age once did – though in a rather more sophisticated way.

As you'll see, there have been a good many stages in between.

1 Once more into the red, dear friends

Sextus Pompilius was a Roman legionary with a headache. It wasn't so much the forced marches and the hordes of barbarians as the problem of money, or rather the lack of it.

He wanted promotion. But would he be able to afford the new equipment when promotion came? Half his pay was already docked by the ensign for his pension, and he was no longer on the best of terms with his banker. Luckily for Sextus there were others in the same boat. They put their heads together and dreamt up a scheme.

And so we learn that in AD 203 a mutual club called 'The Hornblowers' was formed in the Roman garrison town of Lambaesis in Algeria.

Its members, all legionary officers, paid monthly contributions into a big central kitty. And on those particular occasions when a member needed cash, the kitty would provide it:

> 500 *denarii* on promotion
> 500 *denarii* on transfer (plus travel expenses)
> 500 *denarii* when he became a veteran (only 250 if he was degraded or dismissed)
> and 500 *denarii* to his family if he died.

For example, if there was one thing a Roman hated, it was the thought of a slap-dash burial. So a lot of poor people who couldn't afford a decent funeral on their own chose to join a mutual burial club. For a small contribution they ensured a restful eternity for their departed souls.

Not that they were morbid people. In fact, by sharing their meagre funds in these clubs, they showed themselves to be not only rather progressive, but fun-loving too.

We can guess this from the entrance fee to one club at Lanuvium, founded AD 136. Prospective members were asked to bring with them 100 *sestertii* – and an amphora of decent wine.

2 Healthy, wealthy, stealthy and wise

There was another bright idea going the rounds in Rome at that time: an 'immediate annuity' they called it. It was rather like the club idea stood on its head, because with an annuity, instead of making regular payments in return for a cash sum, you pay a cash sum in return for regular payments.

Ever since then, anyone with ready cash to spare has had the chance to buy himself a bargain: like the Archbishop of Bremen did in 1308. This wily old ecclesiastic dangled a sum of 2400 *livres* before the Abbot of St Denis, and proposed a modest annuity. The Abbot took one glance at the Archbishop and marked him down for an early grave. So in return for the 2400 *livres* he agreed to pay out 400 a year for the rest of the Archbishop's life.

The Abbot was obviously hoping to make a tidy profit from the deal. If the Archbishop died in a couple of years he'd stand to gain 1600 *livres*.

To his horror, the Archbishop soldiered merrily on for the next nineteen years. By 1320 the Abbot was finding it hard to sleep at night. In 1323 he tried – unsuccessfully – to contest the contract. When the Archbishop finally passed away in 1327 the Abbot had made a total loss of 5200 *livres*.

(Of course, there's a moral in this tale for every Abbot: before you start to grant your annuities, collect enough Archbishops together to cover your losses.)

A rather endearing, lucky-dip variation on an annuity was a corody. Initially this was a kind of thank-you present from a king or prince to a loyal and faithful servant or a worthy royal chaplain. It gave him the right to certain privileges, such as a candle and straw allowance, and bed and breakfast in a monastery.

Later on corodies could be bought and sold just like annuities, and some quaint and quirky bargains were struck. Lord William of Illebone, for example, having a few fields to spare, parted with them in exchange for a real hotch-potch of an income:

> £10 in money, a robe (10 ells of cloth), two furs, and two capes of budge, three loads of hay, two of straw, three quarters of oats, and two cart-loads of brushwood.

Hordarian's Rolls, 1327-34

It was rather like an exclusive jumble sale, this swapping of land for odds and ends: 'exclusive' because obviously all the peasants were excluded...

3 Don't let poor Nellie starve

It was a tough life for a peasant in the Middle Ages. There you were, a serf right down to your toenails, tilling the soil for your high and mighty Baron, with no freedom and no prospects whatever. The only thing you could take comfort in was your job security and the Baron's protection – he'd make sure nothing stopped your career!

Mind you, going it alone was worse. Try to eke out an independent living as, say, a cobbler, and God help you. God and your fellow cobblers, that is.

Despite all the odds many a poor serf did turn his back on his Baron and open up shop, looking to his fellows for support and encouragement. Alone against the world these brave new cobblers, weavers and tailors began to form little craft clubs, called guilds, where they could meet together and help each other out.

The livelihood of each craftsman and his family hung by a very thin thread. If a cobbler couldn't work, he and his wife would starve. At his death she and her children would face destitution. It became obvious that guild funds were desperately needed for such times of distress. But who was there to pay them but the craftsmen themselves?

And so a system of guild protection was evolved. Each member was asked to contribute a little to his guild's funds. This contribution entitled each one equally to a life-saving loan or subsidy whenever things went wrong: when he fell ill or had no customers; when his wife was poorly or widowed; even when his daughter came of age:

> If any good girl of the guild of marriageable age, cannot have the means found by her father, either to go into a religious house or to marry... friendly and right help shall be given her, out of our means and our common chest, towards enabling her to do whichever of the two she wishes.

Guild of Palmers, Ludlow 1284

A guild's protection was never extravagant: the subsidies were usually counted out in ha'pennies. But it was at least truly comprehensive, lasting from the cradle to well beyond the grave.

4 New life on the ocean wave

Of course there has always been as great a need for short-term as for life-long protection.

Take a fifteenth-century Christian on a trip to the Mediterranean, for instance: he'd have considerable nerve even to contemplate the journey, what with the Turks and Barbary pirates roaming the seas. If his vessel was seized, he'd face a life of slavery or a walk down the plank, unless he could rustle up a ransom. Ever tried rustling up a ransom in mid ocean?

It was a good job there were ransom insurance agents at the dockside. For a small fee, called a premium, a traveller could assure himself of a nice lump sum, if needed, and a welcome rescue from a dreadful end.

In other words, if the pirates didn't appear, his ransom money wouldn't be needed. His premium, together with all the others in the dockside fund, would go towards paying the ransoms of his less fortunate brethren. Whichever way the wind blew, he'd have set his mind at rest.

The same insurance agents could also be offering a traveller a short-term life assurance policy. If he was a debtor, such a policy would do wonders for his money-lender's peace of mind. In fact, behind many of the short-term policies of the fifteenth and sixteenth centuries lurked a cautious Shylock, unwilling to offer a loan, even to a gentleman, without some proof of repayment should his client die.

A client who insured his life for the amount of his loan – to benefit his creditor – was a very welcome proposition. An alternative way round was for the creditor to insure the life of his debtor – once again for his own benefit. In either case, Shylock could then sleep snugly, secure in the knowledge that his money would be returned, no matter what happened.

The earliest written life assurance policy we've been able to find could well have meant a happy ending for a creditor. On 18 June 1583, a London merchant called Richard Martin took out a policy on the life of a certain William Gybbons for a period of twelve months, at a cost of £382 6s. 8d. The insurance men ended the policy with a heart-felt:

God send the said William Gybbons health and a long life.

But William let them down badly, by dying quite perversely just before the twelve months were up – on 9 June 1584.

They felt so vexed by this that they tried to pretend that the twelve-month period actually meant twelve *lunar* months – which had expired before Gybbons had – rather than twelve calendar months.

However justice won the day and they eventually had to pay out. Richard Martin had found himself in good and righteous hands.

5 Drink deep and gamble high

In later, less stable times when insurances proliferated, justice could rarely hope to prevail.

In *Martin Chuzzlewit* Charles Dickens takes the lid off a truly nasty piece of business called the 'Anglo-Bengalee Disinterested Loan and Life Assurance Company'. The only 'disinterest' this organization displays is towards repaying its poor gullible members who 'trust us as if we were the Mint'.

Unfortunately the Anglo-Bengalee, corrupt and swindling as it was, belonged as much to fact as to fiction, because in the late seventeenth and early eighteenth centuries life assurance tottered drunkenly and went off the rails, along with many other financial ventures.

In those reckless, war-torn, gin-filled times ('drunk for a penny, dead drunk for tuppence') gambling or wagering was the order of the day, and you could make and break a fortune in an hour. No branch of insurance could hold out against the gambling mania, and even life assurance in some instances became ludicrously and hopelessly involved in it.

Daniel Defoe exposed the facts in a scathing document written in 1697:

> Wagering...is become a branch of assurance; it was before, more properly, a part of gaming.

Fired by the desire to 'get rich quick', people were actually queueing up to take out insurances on the lives of prominent - and totally unrelated - men and women; on important events in the war; even on the staying power of Louis XV's mistresses.* And when the evil State lottery was introduced they really went to town. Women were seen tearing off and pawning their stockings and petticoats to take out a most unlikely form of insurance meant to guarantee some sort of a prize.

Most of these dubious transactions lasted just long enough to fill the insurer's wallet.

Some companies and 'Friendly Societies' did still struggle to offer genuine protection to their members. This usually took the form of a lump sum payable on a member's death to his family. But since the premiums were largely based on sheer guesswork, and since everyone, regardless of age, contributed the same, these schemes were, to all intents and purposes, as risky as the rest. In order to keep your family's head above water, you had to make sure you died early on, in a 'good year'. Because if you died in a 'bad year', that is, together with a whole lot of others, the funds would be split so many ways that no one would end up with anything worthwhile.

No matter how well-intentioned these groups were, without a solid systematic foundation they were doomed eventually to cause more hardship than they cured.

* 1708 - Parliament forbade all wagering on war.
  1774 - Parliament prohibited life assurance 'except in cases where the person insuring shall have an interest in the life or death of the person insured'.

6 If at first you don't succeed

In 1756 a mathematician called James Dodson was refused a life assurance policy by the Amicable Society on account of his age. When they could get the £7 10s. entrance fee plus £5 annual premium from a strapping young lad, a doddering oldster like him was an unwelcome threat to their funds.

Dodson was 46 at the time.

In a fit of pique he set to work on his own life assurance plan. It had to be a fair one with a rock-solid foundation, available to everyone. It would have to take into account the age of each member as he entered the scheme, and the length of time he remained there.

Dodson studied a lot of tombstone detail – all the records of births and lifespans he could lay hands on. Then he battled with probabilities in a long series of complex sums. (He was used to this sort of thing – his first published work was a pretty impressive tome on anti-logarithms.)

What he eventually came up with is the systematic and scientific basis of life assurance as it is today. It is in fact a highly refined version of our old friend the 'group'.

Each member of Dodson's group would assure his life for a certain sum of money over a certain number of years. This sum was guaranteed to be paid out whenever he died, or when he reached a certain age. All he had to do was to pay a level yearly premium, calculated according to his age and assurance period.

This scientifically calculated level premium idea was a real world-shaker. What Dodson had done was to average everything out. Not only had he spread his combined risks fairly over his entire group. He had also spread each member's individual risk over his entire insurance period: the higher cost of insuring his later years had been balanced out by the lower cost of insuring his earlier years.

The guesswork gone, life assurance had at last become a viable proposition. It would be affordable - even for an old pensioner of 46, though he'd pay more than his son - and it would be safe, the members themselves owning the fund they built up.

But fate dealt Dodson a barrage of blows. He actually died before his Society - the Equitable - was formed. The Society itself nearly bit the dust too. Because of its cheap-sounding premiums it was considered a hare-brained scheme and refused a Royal Charter. And then the public, for many of whom a life policy was tantamount to an admission of poverty, simply stayed away.

Eventually, however, the scheme paid off, and by 1776 it was going great guns. In fact the surplus of £25 142 declared in that year exceeded so many expectations that a hefty £11 000 was doled out as cash bonuses to the delighted policyholders.

Far from being inadequate, the premiums had proved exorbitant, due to the fact that Dodson, in working out his tables, had had to grapple with some rather unusual eighteenth-century factors such as pestilence, gin-drinking and bad winters. A clear 10 per cent was then knocked off his figures.

Even Charles Dickens, who could always spot a good thing when he saw one, changed his contemptuous attitude towards life assurance. On 19 November 1841 he took out a policy with the Eagle, one of the Equitable's later competitors, for the sum of £5000.

On his death in 1870, after a succession of bonuses had been added to this amount, his beneficiaries were graced with the truly princely figure of £6337 7s.

7 'I do not want to be insured. I have made up my mind not to die, even for a profit'

The peasant in William Saroyan's story 'The Insurance Salesman, the Peasant, the Rug Merchant, and the Potted Plant'

So far life assurance has had a very definite personality. It's been a great big guardian angel swooping down in the hour of need, saving Sextus from the red, the Archbishop from a bleak old age, Nell from the workhouse, and a good few heirs from the breadline.

How do you reconcile this protective guardian angel image with the present fairy godmother approach: the fact that nowadays life assurance seems to be concerned more with retirement incomes, mortgage repayments and world cruises than with life cover?

The whole business completely baffled Saroyan's peasant. And it seems to get more complicated daily, not to mention downright suspect.

The explanation is simply that life assurance consists of two different elements.

It's still on the side of the angels. In fact no one can offer you and your family anything like its protection.

But, along with every other financial transaction these days, life assurance has become investment-conscious. You see, what with inflation, slumps and recessions, it makes ever-increasing sense to put aside tuppence today with the promise of fourpence tomorrow. Fourpence for your family if you die, yes of course. But even better, fourpence for your pains if you don't.

Since life assurance has always been flexible enough to move with the times, it's now come to form a large part of our modern investment industry. By popular request, as it were, it's joined the ranks of fairy-godmothers, offering new money for old.

What's more, to popular acclaim, it's making a great success of its new role, owing to the advantage it has (in most cases) over other savings-type schemes: a two-time tax treat. Not only do you pay no income tax on what comes out of your policy, you get tax relief on what goes in.

Guardian angel and fairy godmother, protection and investment, you'll meet them both in the next few chapters, though not necessarily hand in hand.

8 Your money or your life

That globe-trotting Christian from Chapter 4 paid out a premium before he set sail, and never saw it again – unless something happened to him. His premium bought him peace of mind if Fate was kind, and the life-saving cash if it wasn't.

Now how does the following scheme compare?

A man insures his life to the tune of, say, £10 000, to benefit his family. For a set number of years he pays out premiums. His family gain nothing from them – unless he dies within that period. His premiums buy him peace of mind if Fate is kind, and the life-saving cash for his family if it isn't.

If these are very similar situations it is because this simplest form of life assurance, called *term* assurance, is a protection-only scheme: a protection against death, just as another type of insurance might be a protection against pirates, or baggage loss, or perhaps a car accident.

Term assurance is the cheapest way any breadwinner can protect his dependants – over a set period of time – against the financial loss his death would cause them. In other words, it ensures that if his family can't have his life, they can at least get something like his replacement value in money.

So far so good. Funereal, but quite intelligible. Unfortunately the path of true life never has run that smooth. There's a need, is there not, for different amounts of protection at different stages in one's life. Maximum protection, for example, coinciding with the first flush of marital bliss: when there's a 90 per cent mortgage to pay off, all too little to be earned, and three prospective under-fives to feed and clothe. Continuing high protection as the children – and their appetites – develop. Then less and less cover as the wages go up and the kids begin their paper rounds.

Insurance companies, gauging this need, dreamt up a variation on term called *decreasing term* assurance.

There are different types of decreasing term assurance, but they all have in common a very low premium rate. For a 30-year-old man over a twenty-year term this would be around £1 a month for every £1000 assured, as opposed to £1.50 in an ordinary or level term scheme. Because his life cover is decreasing year by year in line with his family's financial needs at his death, his average cover over the years is lower, and his premiums are therefore reduced.

You can see how much sense decreasing term assurance makes if you're in the middle of repaying a loan like a mortgage. Every year you owe a little bit less of your loan, so every year your family need less in the way of protection. Take out a decreasing term assurance called a *mortgage protection policy* linked to the amount and repayment period of your loan, and in the event of your death they should get just exactly the money they need to pay off the remaining debt. That is, unless your interest rate is changed – a point worth discussing with your adviser.

Of course all these schemes apply as much to women as to men, particularly in the case of a one-parent mother-only family, or an earning couple with a joint mortgage. What is often overlooked is that, when it comes to providing for one's family, a non-earning wife plays a vital financial role too.

Let's say the mortgage debt is covered now; how are the family going to live?

If the breadwinning husband or wife dies, the consequences are obvious: there'll be a big drop or total loss in the family income. But if a housewife and mother dies there'll still be a serious money problem. The husband will either have to fork out for a housekeeper for the children, or take a cut in his salary in order to spend more time with them himself.

This is the reason why a *family income benefit policy* is particularly right for both parents in a family, whether they're earning or not. Here's how it works.

Over the term agreed you pay out a small monthly (or yearly) premium. If you should die during the term, your family would get a prearranged income, say £3000 a year, payable three-monthly, right up to the end of the term. The explanation for the cheap premiums here is that, for every year that you staunchly keep on living, the insurance company is saving itself another £3000.

All very well, you may say, but it's a shame there couldn't be just one type of term assurance with just one little hint of investment tucked in somewhere.

Well in point of fact there is. For the would-be investor who can't afford to splash out on a savings plan just yet, there's an ingenious scheme around called *convertible term* assurance.

At first this works just like an ordinary or level term assurance: the premiums are low, and there is a lump sum payable at death. However, it gives the policy-holder the option later on of swapping over to an investment type of policy if he feels so inclined. Not only can he 'convert' his policy whenever he wants to during its term, he can do so whatever his state of health.

He gets all the cover he needs immediately, but postpones his decision on what sort of permanent cover he'd like until he feels the time is ripe.

The only problem with term assurance is that terms eventually expire...

9 Anything for a quiet life

This problem doesn't arise with *whole-life* assurance. As its name suggests, this is a life-long scheme. What it does, basically, is put your mind at rest by providing for your family whenever your death occurs. They'll get a lump sum to cover their loss even if you plough on heartily to 103.

Because the protection is so permanent, the premiums for whole-life are higher than for term policies. But there's usually a choice as to how long you pay these premiums which affects your yearly outlay.

You can either opt for paying them until you reach a certain age, say 65, or carry on cheerfully for the rest of your life. This second way obviously works out cheaper: people live so long these days that the insurance company will expect many more premiums from someone who plumps for payment until the very end.

At first you might have a few qualms as to whether you'll be able to afford premiums after you retire. But the way inflation seems to be going, chances are that, by the time you give up work, that premium will seem ludicrously low. Even if you're pushing 40 now.

To complicate things – in the nicest possible way – most whole-life policies sold these days are *with-profits*. This means that, for a slightly bigger premium, you can buy for your family not only the guaranteed payment, which is known as the *sum assured,* but also a share in your insurance company's profits.

This works much like it did for the old Equitable's customers back in 1776. The company at that time, finding itself with a whacking great surplus on its hands, distributed a large chunk of this in cash to its policyholders. Mind you, the reason for its healthy cash balance was because it had set its premiums far too high, and thanks to healthy competition this could never happen nowadays.

However, companies still make tidy profits as a result of the caution they have to exercise when calculating their outgoings. Their profits come from any excess provision they've made for expenses and mortality, from capital appreciation and unexpectedly high interest rates on their wide-ranging investments, and the extra 'cushion' paid by with-profits investors on which they can fall back in times of depression. A with-profits policyholder therefore stands to make a tidy sum from his scheme.

Once every one to three years, when a company works out its surplus, it distributes a bonus, called a *reversionary bonus,* to every with-profits policyholder. All this mouthful means is that, instead of you getting your bonus doled out in cash, it gets added on, safe as houses, to your sum assured.

Over the years you're likely to get a long succession of bonuses tacked on to this sum. Once they're there, they can never be taken away. So when you finally rest in peace, you can lie back and think of your family getting quite a bit more than they bargained for: not only the sum for which you insured your life, but a great pile of bonuses too.

As you can see, after the first few years you're bound to recoup the extra cost payable on your premium. This makes a with-profits policy very much a permanent investment as well as a permanent protection scheme.

In actual fact, even a *non-profit* whole-life assurance – which at death would pay out the sum assured and not a penny more – has to be regarded as a form of investment. After all, it's 100 per cent certain to be paid out one day. It may be difficult to get enthusiastic about the investment element, owing to the policy's inability to keep pace with inflation, but because of the terrific protection it offers, it's still a reasonable place for your money.

Here are a couple of examples.

If you took out a non-profit policy today, aged 25, and had a fatal accident next week, your family would receive your full sum assured in return for one single premium. (The same thing would happen with a with-profits policy, but the premium would be higher.)

If you took out a non-profit policy today, aged 25, and lived, paying premiums all the while, to the ripe old age of 99, your children would stand to inherit about double what you paid out in the way of premiums. (The difference with a with-profits policy being that your children at your death could be well on the way to a fortune.)

There was only ever one real snag about whole-life assurance. There you were, busily protecting your family, tying up your capital: apparently helpless if disaster struck and you needed cash quickly.

Nowadays you can get round even this one. Almost every insurance company will let you use your whole-life policy as security for a tiding-over loan, once it's been going for two or three years. Even though the loan might be small, in most cases it should help you sort out any temporary panics without jeopardizing anyone's future.

10 Have your cake and eat it

So far the spotlight's been on your family and on protection, rather than investment. It's time the stage was cleared for *endowment assurance.*

The initial mechanics of endowment assurance are nothing new. Just as you did with a term policy, you choose the sum of money for which you want to insure your life, and the length of time the policy will run. But then you start to look around extra carefully before crossing any roads. Because once your time period is up, the money all comes to you.

In the majority of cases* you should go for an endowment *with-profits* policy – sharing in the company's prosperity and reaping a steadily increasing crop of bonuses. What you eventually end up with should be a fair old nest-egg.

This seems like a bargain, until you notice that your premium is up again. Depending on your age and policy period, it could be as little as one-third higher than your whole-life premium for the same sum assured, or as much as eight times that amount.

* In fact, such are the rewards of a with-profits scheme, that the non-profit alternative has to be considered a bad buy in comparison.

Despite appearances, this should not worry you unduly. You see, only a very small portion of your premium is put aside by your insurance company to buy you protection. Even so it's enough to guarantee, should anything happen to you, that the full sum assured plus all the bonuses to date goes straight to your family.

All the extra you're paying out gets saved for your future:it'll actually come back to you one day. What's more, it'll be looking much healthier than when you sent it off to work for you.

How much healthier will depend on your age and the company you choose. But, unless you're getting on a bit, a good company, investing your premiums over a ten-year period, should be talking about a net 10 per cent or so a year on your premiums.

However, the true beauty of endowment assurance is that it is as flexible as it is profitable. You can plan for your *maturity date* - the day your money falls due - to coincide with all sorts of events.

Retirement is one: splurge the lot on a round-the-world cruise, or buy yourself a comfortable annuity.

A career break is another: after ten years of saving, a girl could afford to luxuriate for a while. And since women on average live longer than men - about six years longer in fact - their premiums are a little bit cheaper.

You can choose your child's 21st if you like. Most companies run a scheme called a *child's deferred assurance* which lets you hand over your policy's benefits to your child (or nephew, godson, etc.) when he traditionally comes of age. Up to that time you pay the premiums on your own life assurance quite normally, but once he's 21 the rewards are his. He can either take the cash sum with all its bonuses, or take out his own life assurance at a reduced premium rate, whatever the state of his health (sometimes a combination of these alternatives). He even gets these options if you die before his birthday.

Then how about your child's education? A proud new father hoping to send his son to his old school might well have qualms about the fees. The parents of a bright first-former will perhaps have trouble affording their part of his university grant. In both cases a ten- or fifteen-year *educational policy* would alleviate the financial burden.

The money due at maturity is usually paid out in a series of instalments spread over the fee-paying or grant-contribution period. Should the policyholder die before maturity, however, it becomes payable immediately as a lump sum.

A particularly successful and ingenious use for an endowment policy is a modern house-buying scheme.

Until recently the only alternative to an ordinary building society or local authority mortgage was a straight *endowment mortgage*. With this, you arranged a loan from a building society or insurance company, and bought an endowment assurance for exactly the same time period and sum assured as the loan. Then you made your policy over to the building society or insurance company, so that at maturity – or on your prior death – they would get their loan repaid in one lump sum.

Unfortunately, in addition to your premiums, you also had to pay interest on the full amount of the loan throughout the mortgage period. Admittedly you got tax relief* on this interest and on your premiums, plus life cover, and huge profits at maturity in a with-profits scheme. Nevertheless the whole business was still very costly.

What could be done to lower the price? You couldn't reduce the interest. What you could perhaps do was use those huge profits to help pay off the loan: in other words, make your sum assured lower than the amount of the loan, and let those profits make up the difference, not just provide a surplus.

*See Chapter 14.

And so the *low-cost house-purchase plan* was born. It's cheaper than an endowment mortgage because your endowment sum assured is lower. But because you're gathering bonuses as you go, even a cautious estimate of the sum payable at maturity is that it will exceed your original loan. It could even reimburse you for part of your interest payments.

There's hardly any risk in the scheme. Term assurance cover is included in the package so that, should you die, your full mortgage would be paid off immediately. The only thing that could go wrong is that bonuses might drop so much that they wouldn't be high enough at maturity to pay off all your mortgage. It would need very unusual conditions for this to happen.

If there are two breadwinners in your family you can now arrange to take out a *joint* low-cost house-purchase plan, which would work in exactly the same way as a single policy. If either of you should die, the combination of endowment and term assurance would again provide for the full payment of the loan.

From whichever angle you look at it, endowment assurance gives you the best of both worlds.

11 Have a little flutter

Are you bored with security? If you'd like to add a bit of spice to your life assurance, there's a variety of investment-linked policies on the market nowadays.

Theoretically, these are any kind of savings-type policy whose investment return depends on the performance of a certain fund of money. In other words, what you get out of your savings policy depends on how well it does in the fund where it's invested.

In actual fact it bears a more than passing resemblance to an endowment assurance. However, the insurance companies, instead of spreading your premiums out over a wide range of different investments, generally spread them out over a wide range of similar investments.

The most common sort of investment-linked policy is the unit-linked type. Here the bulk of your premium is used by your company to buy units for you in a unit trust or share fund, a 'managed' fund, or a property fund – the favourite being the unit trust, either managed by the company itself or by a separate body.

The unit trust version is called *equity-linked* assurance, because a unit trust is a collection of different company shares or equities.

Here's what happens. Your company puts aside part of your premium to buy your life cover and pay any expenses. With the rest it buys, on your behalf, a certain number of units in a unit trust. These units will go up and down in value roughly in line with the fortunes of the stock market. Sometimes you can even chart their progress in the papers.

However, their day-to-day performance doesn't affect you so much as their value at maturity – when your policy comes to an end. Their value at maturity is in fact what you get out of an equity-linked policy. If your particular unit trust proves successful, it's going to do you proud.

You may wonder why you don't just go off and invest direct in a unit trust yourself. The reason is twofold. Firstly, in addition to the return on your units, you're going to get that life cover already mentioned: the same sort of protection you'd get in a straight endowment assurance. Secondly, because of the way tax relief works,* you'll get more of your money invested through a life assurance scheme than if you invest direct.

Before you rush out and buy your equity-linked policy, there are a few points to ponder.

Unfortunately no one can predict the value of your units at maturity – don't forget this could easily be twenty years hence. Present factors seem to indicate that your units should prosper, even that your investment could outstrip inflation, but it's still possible that you could end up with a fairly meagre deal.

*See Chapter 14.

56

There are ways of guarding against disappointment at maturity. Most companies these days offer safeguards of one sort or another. Many guarantee a minimum sum at maturity: never less than the total premiums you've paid out over the years. Some also allow you to leave your ailing units in the fund after maturity (although you stop paying premiums) in the hope that the stock market will soon pick up.

There are ways, too, in which you can protect your interests in advance. You can go for a reliable, wide-ranging, well-established fund of shares with a good investment record (although even a brilliant track record can't guarantee future success). You can find out exactly how much of your premium is going to be invested for you after all charges and deductions have been made. You can check whether the yearly income from your investment is reinvested for you, and whether the company deducts any further expenses from the value of your units at maturity.

If all this seems like one big headache, you could try to reduce your risks by buying units in a *managed* fund. This would contain a combination of shares, property and government stocks, and would usually be run by the insurance company itself. It would in fact be a fair approximation of a conventional life assurance fund, but instead of getting bonuses you would again get the value of your units at maturity.

Alternatively you could opt for the relative stability of a *property* fund. This is the only way the average person can participate in the possible profits of this sometimes lucrative field. Provided you ensure that you're buying a stake in a well-run fund, containing property of all types in different geographical locations, you can be pretty sure of a steady increase in price of your bricks and mortar, and correspondingly of your units.

Other people's property may fail to excite you. But if your own dream house is another matter, you could do very well out of a slight oddity called a *building-society-linked* (or *bank-linked*) investment scheme.

This is the way this one works. Most of your premium is invested by your company in a building society (or bank) account. The consequence of tax relief* is that you end up with more money invested this indirect way than if you went straight to the building society itself. Although the rate you get on your savings is below the normal building society rate, you'll find that you get a remarkably good return on your money if you keep it in the scheme for four or five years and then cash it in: normally the last measure you should ever resort to.

What's more, you get in addition what amounts to free life cover, plus the same priority for a mortgage as you'd get by investing direct.

*See Chapter 14.

12 Fates worse than death

While we're considering oddities, it's worth mentioning the fact that some policies issued by life assurance companies have nothing to do with death.

This may not surprise you: as you've already seen, life assurance is very much more about life than death. It's a way of providing the economic wherewithal to live life to the full, in spite of fate. And death is not necessarily fate's cruellest blow.

Imagine a married man with three young children and a long-term mortgage. One day he's hit by a car, and the next he's in a wheelchair.

Maybe his employer is sympathetic and continues his pay for a month or two. But after that it could be one long downhill struggle. The whole family will suffer if he can't go back to work. And even if his wife's employed the house will have to go.

Amidst all this gloom and doom shines the welcome light of a *permanent health insurance* scheme. This provides a weekly income for you if through sickness or accident you are unable to work. You choose the income you'd like and the length of time the policy will last. Then you select a *deferment period*: the number of weeks you can afford to be 'resting' before you start receiving payments. This could be 4, 13, 26 or 52 weeks. The longer your deferment period, the cheaper will be your premiums.

If you regularly climb Everest – or down a pint of Scotch a day – you may find yourself excluded from the scheme. But normally, in return for regular premiums, you will be entitled to your weekly income 4, 13, 26 or 52 weeks

after you first fall ill. What's more, this income will continue for as long as your incapacity lasts, right up to the final day of the policy.

There are two tiny snags. The first is that there is no tax relief on the premiums you pay. And secondly, women have to pay something like one and a half times the premium of a man of the same age engaged in the same occupation. Statistically, it seems, women are ill more often than men.

Nevertheless, for many a self-employed or family man who simply can't afford to be ill, a permanent health insurance scheme represents his only hope in sickness of ever salvaging a decent standard of living. How else will he keep himself and his family in the style to which they've become accustomed?

This is a question he might ask himself again at retirement. The drop in income at retirement can affect people's lives very badly. You may have all the time in the world to do all the things you've ever wanted to do, but it's no fun if you have to think twice before shelling out for a paper or a round of drinks in the pub.

Even if you've got a little capital – or one of those gold watches to pawn – chances are you couldn't live off the interest. Worse, you could outlive the capital, and be left with nothing but a long stretch of useless old age.

Here's where annuities come into their own. If that lump sum's there for the asking, you can still do as the wily Archbishop did and buy yourself an *immediate annuity* once you leave work. You'll ensure a regular income straight away that goes on being paid for the rest of your life. It's an excellent way not only of rationing out your resources, but of inflating them beyond all expectation, should you live to receive your Queen's telegram. Even women, who get a poorer deal than men on annuities since they live that much longer, should find them well worth their while.

Let's face it though, you may be thinking: anyone who's got a cash sum hasn't really got a cash problem.

Well, there's an answer for the rest of us too. Nowadays

you can buy something called a *deferred annuity* from a life assurance company. Instead of paying a lump sum, you contribute regular payments over a number of years, and start to receive your annuity at the end of that time.

Does this type of scheme ring any bells? It is in fact the basis of almost all the pension schemes you'll come across. Annuities, when all's said and done, really mean the same as pensions.

Life companies do a tremendous trade in pensions: for groups and businesses as well as for individuals. The choice of options is incredibly wide, even within a single company.

To keep up with inflation, pensions can share in companies' profits or be unit-linked. They can increase in value at a fixed rate each year or remain constant. They can even continue to pay out after a pensioner's death if he dies before his prearranged term is up.

What's more, life offices provide all sorts of additional services related to pensions, such as help for a widow, or for a man who leaves a group scheme.

Of course, you may already be a member of an occupational pension scheme. Many people are – unless they happen to be self-employed.

Until about twenty years ago the self-employed had a pretty poor time of it at the thin end of the pension wedge. Fortunately recent years have seen the birth of a truly flexible and rewarding scheme called a *self-employed retirement annuity.*

In this scheme you pay premiums out of your earned income on which you'll get tax relief at your highest rate of tax. Your insurance company will invest them for you in a tax-free fund. Some time after your sixtieth birthday, when you decide to retire, you'll be able to take a good portion of your benefit as a tax-free cash sum, the rest coming as a pension (taxed as earned income).

You're not allowed to take out this annuity if you happen to be a member of a pension plan already. However, if you take on another job – perhaps in the evenings or at weekends – you can top up your pension with a retirement annuity based on your separate earnings.

Those of you already holding down two jobs at a time could have yourselves a field-day at retirement. Just think of the possibilities: a nice fat pension, or a cash sum plus pension, from job number one, and a tidy little nest-egg plus an income from job number two.

13 Bespoke, made-to-measure, and ready-to-wear

If it seems as though we're wallowing in a great sea of policies, here's where we put an end to the life assurance roll-call and settle down to specifics.

If you've already identified with five or six policies, you have every right to be flummoxed. Say you'd like to protect your mortgage and see to your family, but you also rather fancy some kind of investment, not to mention a pension scheme and a bit of permanent health insurance. Where on earth do you begin?

When it comes to the nitty-gritty, there are three main factors to bear in mind. Firstly, your particular needs at different stages in your life. Secondly, your personal preferences and priorities. And thirdly, the state of your pocket as the years go by.

In order to see how these three factors combine to influence your moves, it's useful to invent a few simple case-histories.

Take an average 19-year-old, for example. Long-term saving is the very last thing he'd be considering. He'd probably laugh at the mere idea of life assurance – unless

he's got a girl on his mind and a plan in his head that calls for protection.

A protection scheme, started when he's young, will cost him next to nothing. For less than £3 a month he could buy £15 000 worth of life cover for thirty years with a convertible term policy. Whenever he wants, perhaps ten years later, he can convert this into a whole-life or endowment policy, more suited to his later needs and resources.

His 25-year-old brother would again look first to
protection. His commitments and rather stretched income
will restrict his options a little. With just a small outlay
available, and a mortgage and family to cover, his best bet
may again be term assurance – a mortgage protection and
a family income scheme.

But he may also feel very strongly about the need for
protection in the event of his wife's death. So personal
choice could lead to them taking out a joint family income

policy, just as it could lead perhaps to a joint annuity scheme for them later on in life.

How about his 30-year-old neighbour? He might opt for whole-life assurance now, with a view to supplementing this later with an equity-linked savings plan. To protect his family if he falls ill, he might also feel that a permanent health insurance scheme is a must.

Meanwhile, perhaps, his dear old Dad is over half-way through his savings plan. He'd eventually like an annuity to supplement his pension. But at present he's delighted with his brand new grand-daughter: how about a nest-egg for her 21st birthday?

Modern life assurance, as you can see, is not a choose-one-policy-and-stick-to-it affair. It's a developing programme that ties in with your life: changing, growing, and altering direction in line with you.

This programme will often begin with a term policy, move on to whole-life, and then progress to endowment assurance, if funds permit, ending with an annuity bought with the proceeds at maturity. But this progression won't always be right for everyone. So it's up to you to plan your own to fit your individual needs.

Maybe you're a very special case. You could be just the person for the out-of-the-ordinary policies some companies can offer. If so, how about a ten-year combination scheme: whole-life plus term, or annuity plus endowment joined together? A scheme that offers security for the partners in your business, or one that provides for possible capital transfer tax* liability? Or perhaps a variation on a theme, such as decreasing endowment assurance?

*See Glossary.

Some companies will even design an exclusive policy for a particular requirement. Others cater specially for women. So if you can't make do with off-the-peg, you can try made-to-measure.

Amidst all these choices and personal priorities, it's impossible to lay down cut-and-dried guidelines for every single reader. However, two special points are well worth stressing. They both concern savings policies, because it's hard to blunder with a protection type of policy.

First you should remember that, once your money goes into a savings policy, it's stuck there for a good many years. So don't part with even one premium until you're absolutely positive that you can do without that money for that length of time. If you're unsure as to whether you can or not, try saving the amount of your monthly premium in a building society first. If after a year it's all still there, you can use your savings to start your policy. If you've had to take it out, you'll certainly know where you stand – and in addition you'll have made a tidy gain.

Secondly, it's wise to avoid a non-profit endowment policy, unless you're definitely only going to need a specific, unalterable sum at maturity, or, alternatively, unless you intend to convert it to with-profits within a few years.

You're really losing out on a non-profit scheme, because any surplus a company gets from your premium is going to go straight to a with-profits policyholder in his next bonus. Moreover, because of the high rates of inflation these days, you're sitting on a pretty poor investment.

Any doubts you may have with regard to the smaller amount of life cover you'd be buying with your with-profits premiums can be easily resolved. All you have to do is add a little extra term cover.

14 Sing a song of fivepence

There's been a conspicuous lack of money facts and costings so far.

It's true, of course, that many circumstances determine the size of your premiums: your age and sex, the company you choose, the precise nature and length of the policy, and the future performance of various investments. This explains the absence of charts, graphs and estimates in this book: they'd all be approximate anyway.

The main reason, however, for postponing a look at prices is that what you're asked by your company to pay is practically never what you actually end up by paying. The reason stems from one of life assurance's great assets: tax relief.

Life offices have to pay tax on the investment profits they make-for your benefit-on their life assurance funds (though not on their pension funds). But you as an individual not only pay no income tax (or capital gains tax) on what comes out of your policy, you also get tax relief on what goes in.

On almost every policy you can get back from the government a percentage of what you pay out each year in

the way of premiums. This percentage equals half the basic rate of income tax, and is currently 17 per cent, the basic rate of tax being 34 per cent. The only policies that don't usually qualify are single-premium ones. When it comes to pensions, you should get tax relief at the highest rate of tax you pay.

There are some inevitable provisos for the half-the-basic-rate rule, but in practice they're most unlikely to affect you.

The policy has to be for a term of at least ten years. It must be taken out on your own or your better half's life. And if your total premiums amount to more than one-sixth of your income, the extra is not eligible for relief.

At present the tax relief drill goes like this. Your insurance company gives you a certificate to show the Inland Revenue, called a Life Assurance Premium Certificate. You then have to send it off the the tax-man who subsequently adjusts your tax coding.

However, as from April 1979, the tables will be turned, and the insurance companies will have to do the claiming. Instead of your paying the full price of your premiums and getting the percentage discount separately, you'll simply pay the reduced price straight to the company. This will be call a *net premium*.

Tax relief on any kind of premium is welcome. But on a premium for an investment-linked policy it has a special significance: it can actually allow you to invest more money by going through a life office than you ever could by investing directly. What's more, you'd be getting life cover into the bargain.

Unlikely as this may sound, it's not that difficult to follow.

Say you've decided to take out a fifteen year equity-linked endowment policy. The monthly premium is £10. From this £10 your company will first deduct a small amount, say 75p, for your life cover and other expenses. With the rest it will buy, on your behalf, a number of units in a unit trust. So you've got £9.25 invested for your future.

Meanwhile, however, for each month that you pay out £10, you're getting your percentage refund from the tax-man. At the present rate of 17 per cent tax relief you'd have £1.70 returned to you. So you'd really only be paying out £8.30.

See what this means?

You're paying out £8.30 and getting £9.25 invested for you. In addition you're getting life cover thrown in for nothing. It may sound weird, but it really works.

There's another factor too that could affect your investment: it concerns the different types of life assurance company you'll come across today.

Like the Equitable, most early life offices were *mutual* societies or co-operatives. They were owned by their policyholders, who had all the rights to the funds they built up, and any benefits coming from the funds.

Later, limited companies were formed and owned by shareholders to provide life assurance for other people. These were called *proprietary* companies. As each shareholder had helped to build up the capital for the scheme, he naturally expected a return on his investment.

It is this return that concerns the man in the street. Since a mutual office is owned by its policyholders, every penny of its net profit belongs to those in with-profits schemes. A proprietary company however has to split its profits two separate ways. Some (no more than 10 per cent) has to go to the shareholders before the rest can get paid out as bonuses.

It's a point worth bearing in mind when you get round to choosing your company.

15 Eeny, meeny, miny, mo

Just how do you get round to choosing your life assurance company though? Do you stick a pin in the Yellow Pages or take pot luck with an honest-sounding salesman?

It's no problem with *industrial* life assurance. This is a special 'home service' available in many areas, where an agent comes knocking at your door, perhaps once a month. You don't have to lift a finger, except to hand him your premium. Although the range of policies offered is a little restricted – and the prices are a little higher – you still get all the usual perks like bonuses, plus a word in your ear if you need some advice.

Otherwise it's a matter of sending off the coupons in insurance company ads, or braving the law of the jungle: that forest of salesmen, accountants, bankers and brokers, all vying for your custom.

Let's try to see the wood despite the trees. What exactly do these people offer? What's in it for them? Can anyone be trusted? Who gives the best deal?

Imagine a salesman first, of the door-to-door sort. He's probably working for a particular company. So what he offers are his particular company's policies.

Now, provided both he and his company are reputable, you're in good hands here. The chances are he'll spend a lot of time and care over your case and come up trumps with a plan that's just right for you.

What's more, he'll provide a thoughtful, thorough (and free) 'after-sales service', popping round when you need him with everything from tax advice to benefit cheques. It's your interests alone that concern him, not his own rewards. After all, he has his company's reputation to uphold.

You might just occasionally strike unlucky though. A more unscrupulous salesman out for a big commission could do you a mischief. He might plug a savings plan when you only need protection – his cut is that much bigger. He might quote bonus figures you'll never see on paper. Or promise you a mortgage that'll never see the light. His potential gain is your potential loss.

There are so many safeguards nowadays, designed to protect the public, that life assurance has become a tremendously secure business. For example, most life offices belong to associations formed to maintain high standards by laying down certain regulations, such as maximum commission rates. And all life offices have to submit details of their business before the critical eyes of the Department of Trade.

There are however a few extra precautions you could take to protect yourself. It's wise to choose a company that's a member of The Life Offices' Association or Associated Scottish Life Offices. It's unwise to believe anything that's not put down in black and white. When it comes to estimates, look at them carefully, making sure you're comparing like with like. And last but not least, if you're unsure, don't go ahead. Always seek further advice before committing yourself to anything.

What further advice? Well, advice comes from all quarters: from your solicitor perhaps, or your accountant; from your bank manager or estate agent; from a friend, even, or a friend of a friend.

Unfortunately you can't always be sure this advice is sound and unbiased. What's right for a friend of a friend, for example, may not necessarily be right for you.

Help could be at hand in the form of an insurance broker. His commission, like the salesman's, is included in your premium, so you pay no fee for his advice.

A good insurance broker with a thorough knowledge of life assurance could do more for you even than a good salesman. The difference between them is this: a broker is not tied to any one company. He can pick the right policy for you from a huge range of schemes offered by all sorts of different companies, including those who don't employ door-to-door salesmen.

Because there are good points and weaknesses in every life office, a good broker can ensure you get the very best deal from a variety of similar packages. In fact he could make your money go that little bit further by comparing and contrasting different premiums and rates of return.

However, good brokers, sad to say, don't grow on trees. In fact not every good broker even belongs to the British

Insurance Brokers' Association. But if you're stuck for expert help and unbiased advice, it's a very good place to contact. Just write to the BIBA at Fountain House, 130 Fenchurch Street, London EC3M 5DJ (Tel.: 01-623 9043), and ask them to recommend a broker in your area.

Of course, no matter whom you get your policy through, the procedure's much the same.

First comes the *proposal form:* a list of questions for you to answer about yourself and your policy. They cover such things as your age, occupation and medical history, and are there simply to provide the company with the information it needs to work out your premium: they don't bind you to anything at all.

To go with this form you'll need a copy of your birth certificate, but normally no medical examination. You'd only have one of these – at the company's expense – if you were over a specified age (usually 55), had a history of illness, or were insuring your life for a great deal of money.

Next comes the *acceptance letter.* If a company accepts you as a future policyholder, they send you a letter stating your premium rate and the basic details of the contract. If you don't like the look of this you're still not bound to go ahead.

It is only when you accept the details in the letter and pay your *first premium* (usually monthly or yearly) that the contract is complete and you have to stick by its terms.

This is when the company sends you your *policy document.* Here the full details of your contract – including the benefits you're going to get – are all set out. It's a valuable document, and you should read it, making sure you understand it, before putting it away in a safe place. It will have to be produced whenever a claim is made on it.

A claim is made by filling in a *claim form*; *death* or *maturity benefit* being the sum payable when that claim comes through.

If the claim follows a death, the life office will ask to see a copy of the death certificate and any other relevant documents. Unfortunately the money doesn't always arrive immediately afterwards, and there could be problems as to where it eventually goes, if the policyholder died without making a will.

It's important therefore to consult your adviser as to what would happen in your particular case. Ask whether anything can be done to speed the money through, and ascertain exactly who will benefit. It could save you or others a great deal of heartache in the future.

16 Ironing out the creases

You can happily assume that nine times out of ten this whole process will be smooth, efficient and trouble-free. However, every now and then there are things that go bump in your life which could threaten your policy.

The prime example is a panic over money. Suddenly, you can't afford to pay your premiums. Worse, you need back all the money you've paid out. Danger, you rush off and cancel your policy. Result, you land yourself in even deeper water.

Cancelling your policy at any time is almost always the worst step you can take. Far from a decent return on your premiums, you'll get only a proportion of their value. The exact amount you receive, the *surrender value*, depends of course on all sorts of circumstances. But as an example, if you cashed in your whole-life policy after paying out regularly for as long as thirty years, you'd not get more than half your sum assured.

Apart from that oddity, the building society-linked policy, there's only one exception to this watertight rule. It's called a *flexible endowment*. It's the only policy where you don't decide beforehand when you want it to mature: you just pay out the premiums until you need the money back. But even a flexible endowment (which costs more than a fixed-length endowment) has to be kept up for a minimum of ten years.

So is there any way out of this need-money-quick quandary? In actual fact there are two.

The first is to 'freeze' your policy by making it *paid-up*. This means that you stop paying premiums, but you don't cash anything in. Your policy is still kept going, but it's now worth less. Your sum assured has been reduced – taking into account the number of premiums you've already paid. However, with some companies it will gradually start to grow again, as bonuses will still get tacked on as usual on an appropriately reduced scale.

If you don't want to reduce your sum assured, or if your financial embarrassment is just temporary, you could try for a loan. You will probably get one from your insurance company or bank, provided your policy has been going for two or three years. Your policy will stand security (or collateral) for your loan: in other words, if you find you can't repay it, the company or bank takes the amount of loan from your policy. Most insurance companies will lend you up to 90 per cent of the surrender value of your policy, at a market rate of interest.

Of course your problem might hit you earlier on. Before you're even granted a policy in fact. Especially if you're a wall-of-death rider with a mild touch of palsy; even if you're an oil rigger with the odd bout of asthma: in other words, a bad insurance risk.

A bad insurance risk might be prompted to keep the fact of his obesity/gout/dizzy spells out of his proposal form. Or he might blithely assume that every life office quotes the same rates for a weekend parachutist or a diabetic. He'd be wrong in both cases.

In the first instance his company could cancel his policy outright (usually returning his premiums) if they discover that he's been covering something up. And in the second instance he may find that some companies refuse to insure him or, more likely, charge him an *extra premium* in addition to the standard one.

The way out of this double dilemma is a quick visit to a broker. Luckily there are companies around that are sympathetic to specific bad-risk cases: a broker should be able to fix most people up. They may be charged a little bit extra, but not as much as a non-specialist company might ask. Since the need for life assurance is often most apparent to bad-risk cases, these specialist companies are a real boon for people with dangerous jobs or a history of illness.

It's their widows who might experience this next kind of problem. The hitch here comes at the very end of the life assurance process: after the benefit has been paid out, no less.

Imagine a widow with a large sum of death benefit in the bank. She's weighed down by her grief and the burden of her new financial commitments. Surprising how many 'friends' she suddenly acquires – financial experts to a man, all full of sound business advice. Before she knows where she is, that money's in one of their schemes – and the 'friends' all disappear.

How can she stop this happening?

She's just got to keep her wits about her. Be firm with persistent 'advisers'. Think about future liabilities as well as present debts. And have a good long talk with her bank manager or solicitor about the relative merits of the different possibilities open to her.

If she's still young, the best place for her money may be a building society account. She'll have easy access to it there, plus the interest that accumulates.

If she's an older woman, she may consider buying an annuity. This way she avoids worrying over how much she should spend each year: her capital simply gets paid out to her like a fixed salary.

Of course there'll always be the enterprising lady who fancies a £5000 gamble on the commodity market – but that's another story.

Glossary

For further information on each entry, try the page(s) mentioned.

ACCEPTANCE: When a company accepts you as an insurance
   risk, it sends you an acceptance letter showing your premium
   and the basic contract details. You're not bound by the contract
   at this stage. See page 80.

ACTUARY: A mathematics expert who calculates life assurance
   premiums and bonuses. He has to juggle with investment returns
   and company expenses as well as death rates.

ANNUITANT: The person to whom an annuity is paid. See page 62.

ANNUITY: An income, usually payable for life, that you can buy
   yourself, either with a single premium lump sum, or a series of
   premiums. In the case of a single premium payment it can be
   immediate - starting straight away after your payment.
   Otherwise it is *deferred* - starting after a certain period of time
   has elapsed. In most cases it is treated as a 'purchased life
   annuity', and only part of your income is taxable (the interest,
   not the capital repayment). Annuities can also be arranged on
   a *joint* basis for a couple. Here the income continues for the rest
   of both their lives. Annuities are the basis of all pension schemes.
   See page 62.

ASSIGNMENT: If you assign your policy to someone, by selling it
   to him or as a gift, he acquires all the policy's benefits. If you
   assign it as security for a loan, his rights are restricted to the
   amount of the loan.

ASSURANCE: Strictly speaking, 'assurance' covers what will
   happen, and 'insurance' covers what may happen. Since no one
   speaks strictly any more, you can say 'life assurance' or 'life

insurance' and be equally correct. However, you can't use 'assurance' for any insurance apart from life insurance.

BENEFIT: Death or maturity benefit is the sum of money payable when a claim is made. See page 81.

BOND: A fancy name for a policy, particularly a single premium policy.

BONUSES: Only apply to with-profits policies. Each policyholder shares in his company's profits by getting periodic bonuses added on to his sum assured. *Reversionary* bonuses are added on every one to three years, whenever the company works out its surplus – and each individual's share of this surplus. Reversionary bonuses can be *simple* or *compound*. 'Simple' means that they are based only on the sum assured. 'Compound' means that they are based on the sum assured and also on any previous bonuses already added. An *interim* bonus is added on to a policy that matures before the coming reversionary bonus has been decided. Sometimes a *terminal* or *final* bonus is added on too when the benefit eventually gets paid. See page 46.

BROKER: The middle-man between you and various insurance companies – an independent insurance agent who can sell you a wide range of policies from many different companies. See pages 79 and 84.

BUILDING SOCIETY-LINKED POLICY: A type of investment policy where your premiums are invested by your insurance company in a building society (or bank) account. Because of the way tax relief works, you could get a good return on your money, particularly after four years, plus life cover and mortgage priority too. See page 58.

CAPITAL GAINS TAX: Where life assurance policies are concerned, this tax is only ever payable by the insurance company itself. However, your return will be adjusted to take your company's liability into account. See page 71.

CAPITAL TRANSFER TAX: A tax imposed when capital totalling over £25 000 changes hands by way of gift. If the benefit from your life policy brings your total estate up above this figure, your heir or beneficiary would normally have to pay CTT on it (unless you pay it for him). The main exemptions are as follows:

Gifts to one's spouse are usually not taxable. If you insure your life for the benefit of your spouse, he or she pays no tax on the proceeds.

A variety of specified annual gifts are exempted. You could use this gift allowance to buy child's deferred policies for all your children: they'd pay no tax on the proceeds.

A lower tax rate applies if you pass your assets to your heir or beneficiary more than three years before your death. He or she could provide for the extra tax liability by taking out a three-year term policy on your life (a 'gifts *inter vivos*' policy).

Other policies whose proceeds are free from CTT are those written under the Married Women's Property Act for the spouse or child, or under another simple trust for anyone else, and those taken out by one person on the life of another.

CHILD'S DEFERRED ASSURANCE: A policy taken out for the benefit of a child (not necessarily one's own), usually maturing on his 21st birthday. At this point he can either take a lump sum, or convert the policy to his own at a very good premium rate, no matter what his state of health (sometimes a combination of these alternatives). See page 50.

CLAIM: At death or maturity a claim is made for the benefit due by filling in a company claim form. See page 81.

CLAW-BACK: If you cancel or 'freeze' your policy, you may in certain circumstances be liable for a tax charge.

COMMISSION: The 'cut' taken by company salesmen, brokers and other agents for introducing business to a company. The policyholder actually pays for this in his premium. See pages 78 and 79.

CONVERTIBLE TERM ASSURANCE: A policy providing life cover for a certain number of years. During this time the policyholder can convert it into an endowment or whole-life policy if he wishes, whatever the state of his health. See page 42.

DAYS OF GRACE: If you can't pay your premium when it's due, you're normally allowed thirty days' grace in which to raise it. After this, you start to pay interest, or lose your cover.

DECREASING TERM ASSURANCE: A policy under which the sum assured, payable on death within a certain period, decreases year by year. Nothing is paid out if the life assured outlives the term. See page 41.

DIRECT DEBIT: You can now pay your premiums by direct debit. Each time your premium falls due, your insurance company will instruct your bank to pay the money out of your bank account. This is more common practice these days than the once popular standing order.

ENDOWMENT ASSURANCE: A savings-type policy, under which the sum assured is payable at maturity - after a certain number of years - or at prior death. See page 49.

ENDOWMENT MORTGAGE: A loan on property arranged with an insurance company or building society. The borrower takes out an endowment assurance on his life for the same time period and sum assured as the loan. In addition to paying his premiums (tax relief here), he pays interest to the lender on the full loan (tax relief again). At maturity, or prior death, his sum assured pays off the loan itself. See page 52.

EQUITIES: Another word for ordinary shares. See page 55.

EQUITY-LINKED POLICY: A type of investment policy. Your return depends on the performance of a unit trust - or share fund - in which your company has invested on your behalf. See page 55.

EXTRA PREMIUM: An extra charge on top of the normal premium for poor insurance risks - people with dangerous jobs or pastimes, or a history of illness. See page 84.

FAMILY INCOME BENEFIT: A type of decreasing term assurance. It usually provides a fixed (sometimes increasing) three-monthly income for a family, from the death of a parent (the life assured) to the end of the term agreed. See page 42.

FLEXIBLE ENDOWMENT: An endowment policy, lasting a minimum of ten years, without a fixed maturity date. You may cash it in without penalty any time after the ten years are up. The premiums are higher than for a fixed-term endowment policy. See page 83.

HOME SERVICE INSURANCE: Also called industrial branch insurance. Some companies arrange for agents to go round from door to door, collecting premiums in person, either weekly, fortnightly or monthly. The range of policies offered here is slightly restricted, as are the areas covered by these schemes. See page 77.

INCOME TAX RELIEF: A policyholder paying tax at the normal rate can usually get back from the tax-man a percentage of his total annual premiums, equal to half the basic rate of income tax. To qualify, his policy must normally last at least ten years, and be on his own or his spouse's life. If his total premiums amount to more than one-sixth of his income, the extra doesn't count. Single premium and permanent health insurances are not eligible, but pension premiums normally qualify for tax relief at the policyholder's highest rate of tax. See pages 38, 61 and 71.

INSPECTOR: Another word for a salesman employed by a British life assurance company.

INSURABLE INTEREST: You're not allowed to insure the life of anyone in whom you do not have a definite financial interest (e.g. wife, partner, debtor). This rule dates back to the 1774 Gambling Act which forbade wagering on totally unconnected lives. See page 30.

INVESTMENT-LINKED POLICY: A savings-type policy. Your return depends on the performance of a specified fund in which your company invests on your behalf. It could be a unit trust, a property or 'managed' fund, or even a building society or bank account. See page 55.

LAPSE: If a policyholder fails to pay his premium after the days of grace are up, his policy lapses, or ceases to exist. However, if it has acquired a surrender value, it will usually stay in force for up to a year, and if it still has a value then, it will automatically be made paid-up.

LIFE ASSURED: The person whose life is being insured or covered. This is not always the policyholder himself. It could be his wife, debtor, partner, etc.

90

LIFE COVER: Financial protection against the death of the life assured. With term or endowment assurance, if he dies before a certain time, the company pays out. With whole-life assurance, whenever he dies the company pays out.

LIFE FUND: The premiums paid by policyholders build up to make a life fund. Since this has to pay every claim made on it, it is invested in a wide variety of concerns – government securities, shares, property, loans, commercial enterprises, etc.

LIFE OFFICE: A shorter way of saying 'life assurance company' or 'the life assurance section of a general insurance company.'

LOAN VALUE: The holder of a whole-life or endowment policy can use it as security for a loan, once it's been going for two or three years. The amount of loan may be small, as it is usually 85-90 per cent of the policy's surrender value at that time. See page 83.

LOW-COST HOUSE PURCHASE PLAN: A cheaper version of a with-profits endowment mortgage, linked to a decreasing term assurance. Here the endowment sum assured is less than the loan, the bonuses eventually making up the difference. Interest on the whole loan is payable to the lender, over and above the premium outlay. The addition of term assurance simply ensures the loan is repaid in full if the policyholder dies. Joint low-cost endowment mortgages (e.g. on husband and wife) are often available. See page 53.

MANAGED FUND: A fund, usually managed by an insurance company, containing a combination of shares, property and government stocks. A savings-type policy could be linked to this fund, the investment return depending on the fund's performance. See page 57.

MARRIED WOMEN'S PROPERTY ACT: Policies written under this Act for the benefit of a wife, husband or child have the following advantages if the policyholder dies. The proceeds are payable immediately and protected against his creditors. And, provided he could afford to pay the premiums out of his income, they are normally also free of capital transfer tax.

MATURITY: The day the money due on an endowment policy becomes payable, unless the life assured has previously died. See page 50.

MORTALITY: The rate at which people die. You used to calculate this by reading tombstones, but nowadays it's all done from mortality tables, based on extensive statistics.

MORTGAGE PROTECTION: Almost any life policy can be used to pay off a mortgage on death. A cheap decreasing term assurance can be tailor-made to pay off the exact amount owing at the time of death. However, since it contains no savings element, a whole-life or endowment policy may prove the best value in the long run. See page 41.

MUTUAL COMPANY: A company owned wholly by its policyholders, who are entitled to all its profits. See page 75.

NET PREMIUM: At present a policyholder pays the full price of his premium and gets his tax relief back separately. As from April 1979, his tax relief will be deducted before he pays his premium, which will therefore be net of tax relief. See page 74.

NON-MEDICAL LIMITS: Usually no medical examination is needed before a company issues a policy, up to a certain limit of sum assured. This 'non-medical limit' could go up to £50 000 or more, depending on the company and the policyholder's age. (If he's over 55 he'll probably be given a medical test automatically, at the company's expense.)

ORDINARY BRANCH INSURANCE: Here premiums are not collected from door to door as with industrial branch insurance, but paid direct to the insurance company in cash, by cheque, or by direct debit.

PAID-UP POLICY: A 'frozen' whole-life or endowment policy – the policyholder has stopped paying premiums but not cancelled his policy altogether. His sum assured is therefore reduced, taking into account the premiums he has already paid. See page 83.

PENSION: Usually an income paid from retirement until death. In addition to your State pension, you may be a member of an occupational pension scheme, or choose from a range of self-employed schemes offered by life offices. Pension premiums are generally eligible for tax relief at the policyholder's highest tax rate. See page 63.

PERMANENT HEALTH INSURANCE: A policy which protects the

holder against sickness or disability rather than death (although it's sold by life offices). An agreed number of weeks after the policyholder falls ill (it could be 4, 13, 26 or 52 weeks) he starts to receive a regular income. This is paid until the time when he is able to go back to work, or until the policy expires, whichever is the sooner. Women pay higher premiums than men for the same amount of income. See page 60.

POLICY: The contract made between you and your insurance company. See page 80.

POLICY DOCUMENT: The document outlining the full details of your contract, including your future benefit. The company will send you this after you've paid your first premium. It will have to be produced whenever a claim on it is made. See page 80.

POLICYHOLDER: The person who owns the policy and pays the premiums. He is usually, but not always, the person whose life is assured.

PREMIUM: The payment you make to your company for your life assurance policy. Usually this is a series of monthly or yearly sums, payable over a period of time. NB. A monthly premium works out about 3-5 per cent more expensive than a yearly one. See pages 25 and 34.

PROFITS: A company's profits come from five main sources: any excess provision it has made for expenses and mortality, capital appreciation and unexpectedly high interest rates on investments, and the extra money provided by with-profits investors. See page 46.

PROPERTY FUND: An investment fund, generally covering a variety of different types of property in various geographical areas. This would normally be managed by an insurance company offering savings-type policies whose return would be linked to the fund's performance. See page 57.

PROPOSAL: An application made to a life office for any sort of life assurance policy. Completing the form does not commit you to taking out the policy. See page 80.

PROPRIETARY COMPANY: A company owned by its shareholders, who expect a return from its profits. A proprietary life assurance company pays up to 10 per cent of its profits to its shareholders before the rest is distributed as bonuses among its with-profits policyholders. See page 75.

PROTECTION: This is another word for life cover.

QUALIFYING POLICY: A policy has to fulfil certain conditions in order to qualify for tax relief on the premiums, and exemption from certain charges. In fact, most policies are specially designed to qualify automatically. See page 73.

RETIREMENT ANNUITY: This provides a cash sum and a pension some time after the policyholder's 60th birthday. Anyone who is not a member of an occupational pension scheme can pay premiums for a retirement annuity – up to certain limits – and receive tax relief at his highest tax rate. See page 63.

SALESMAN: Some salesmen sell insurance directly to the general public, calling round to offer advice and personal service. Others 'sell' their company's policies and particular merits to brokers. Apart from his commission, which is included in your premium, you pay nothing for any salesman's service. See page 77.

SELF-EMPLOYED: Nearly all self-employed people should make a point of seeking advice as to their individual tax situation. Policies of particular interest to them include self-employed retirement annuities and permanent health insurance schemes. See pages 62 and 63.

SOLVENCY: One of the most important attributes of the life assurance industry. What it really means is that you can be sure your company will be there to pay when you are due to be paid.

STANDING ORDER: An instruction from you to your bank to pay a regular debt whenever it falls due. Standing orders were once widely used to pay life assurance premiums, but have recently been superseded by the direct debit system.

SUM ASSURED: Generally the sum of money, agreed beforehand, which is to be paid out at death, or at death or maturity in the case of an endowment assurance. In a with-profits scheme, periodic bonuses are added to the sum assured and paid out together with it. In an investment-linked scheme, the amount payable is not fixed, although a minimum sum, such as the total premiums paid, may be guaranteed. See page 46.

SURRENDER VALUE: The amount payable to a whole-life or endowment policyholder who cancels – or 'surrenders' – his contract. If he does this early on, the surrender value is likely to be less than the premiums he's paid, due to the cost of life cover and administrative expenses. In some cases a tax charge is made on surrender, even for qualifying policies. See page 83.

TERM ASSURANCE: A protection-only policy. The sum assured is paid out only if the life assured dies within the term – the agreed time period – of the policy. See page 40.

UNDERWRITERS: The people who assess the risks involved in, and sometimes issue, policy contracts. Used in a loose sense, 'underwriters' can just mean the insurance company.

UNIT-LINKED POLICY: A type of investment-linked policy. Your company buys with your premiums a number of units in an investment fund – it could be a unit trust, or a 'managed' or property fund, either run by them or independent of them. Either way, your investment return depends on the performance of your units, and their eventual value at maturity. See page 55.

UNIT TRUST: A fund of different shares – less risky as an investment than a batch of identical shares. See page 55.

WHOLE-LIFE ASSURANCE: A life-long protection policy, which also incorporates a savings element as it is bound to pay out one day. Premiums are payable throughout one's life, or up to, say, age 65. The sum assured is paid out whenever death occurs. Whole-life policies nowadays are usually with-profits – or sometimes unit-linked – schemes. They can normally also be used as security for a loan from one's insurance company or bank. See page 45.

WITH-PROFITS POLICY: One which entitles the policyholder to a share in the company's profits. This comes in the form of periodic bonuses added to his sum assured, and paid out together with it at death (whole-life with-profits) or at death or maturity (endowment with-profits). See page 46.

WOMEN: Women generally live longer than men. Their premium rates are therefore usually cheaper for the same sum assured, except in the case of annuities where the position is reversed. However, women seem to fall ill more often than men, so a woman's permanent health insurance rate would be about one and a half times that of a man. See pages 41, 61 and 62.

About the authors

Author and illustrator both came to the subject of Life Assurance as complete innocents. In response to a smokescreen of jargon they decided to pool their talents and create a guide which was at once simple and entertaining.

Tessa Morrison is a graduate in Modern Languages of Newnham College, Cambridge. Grand-daughter of the legendary G. E. Morrison, Peking Correspondent of *The Times*, she has at twenty-eight established a reputation as a writer, researcher and theatre publicist. Following in the family tradition, she plans to live and work abroad, in Aix-en-Provence.

Arthur Robins is thirty-four and has been illustrating books and magazines for the past twelve years. His work has delighted millions. This is the first time he has collaborated with Tessa Morrison. He lives in Cranleigh, Surrey, with his wife and two daughters and is fully covered.